"Finally, a book on the pastor search process which combines the spiritual and the practical! Blackaby and Fisher have put together solid wisdom and good advice for churches who find themselves seeking a new pastor complete with helpful guidance for prayer, procedures, and interviewing potential candidates. I highly recommend it!"

– Dr. David Johnson, Executive Director, Arizona Southern Baptist Mission Network

"Christ loves His Church and will lead it to thrive, if it will heed His guidance. This book provides practical, biblical, and wise counsel for churches making one of their most important decisions. It reflects what I have taught over the years and I know it will bless those who use it."

– Dr. Henry Blackaby, author of *Experiencing God*

"*Your Next Pastor* is an excellent resource for churches and Pastor Search Teams seeking their next spiritual leader and under shepherd. This guide simply and clearly identifies the basics for the journey of seeking God's pastor for your church. Richard Blackaby and Rick Fisher have put together the best resource I've seen on this most important topic."

– Johnny Rumbough, Executive Director/AMS, Lexington Baptist Association

"As someone who has assisted many search committees, I can't recommend this book highly enough. The pastor search process need not be difficult or filled with anxiety. I urge you to allow this resource to encourage and equip you in seeking God's direction."

– Ken Allen, Director of LeaderCare – Alabama State Board of Missions

YOUR NEXT PASTOR

A GOD-CENTERED GUIDE FOR PASTOR SEARCH COMMITTEES

Richard Blackaby
with Rick Fisher

Blackaby Ministries International

Jonesboro, Georgia

YOUR NEXT PASTOR: A GOD-CENTERED GUIDE FOR PASTOR
SEARCH COMMITTEES
PUBLISHED BY BLACKABY MINISTRIES INTERNATIONAL
P.O. Box 1035
Jonesboro, GA 30237
www.blackaby.org

ISBN: 978-1-7350872-5-2

Library of Congress Control Number: 2022909085

Title Page vector created by d3images - www.freepik.com

Publisher's Cataloging-in-Publication Data

Names: Blackaby, Richard, 1961-, author. | Fisher, Ricky, author.

Title: Your next pastor : a God-centered guide for pastor search committees / Richard Blackaby with Rick Fisher.

Description: Jonesboro, GA: Blackaby Ministries International, 2022.

Identifiers: LCCN: 2022909085 | ISBN: 978-1-7350872-5-2

Subjects: LCSH Clergy--Appointment, call, and election. | Pastoral search committees. | Christian leadership. | BISAC RELIGION / Christian Church / General | RELIGION / Christian Church / Administration | RELIGION / Christian Ministry / Pastoral Resources | RELIGION / Clergy | RELIGION / Leadership

Classification: LCC BV664 .B53 2022 | DDC 262.14--dc23

Printed in the United States of America
2022 — 1st ed

Contents

To the many wonderful churches who are earnestly and prayerfully seeking the next pastor for their church.

Christ loves the church with an infinite, eternal love that is beyond our comprehension. The apostle Paul declared that *". . . Christ loved the church and gave himself for her to make her holy, cleansing her with the washing of the water by the word. He did this to present the church to himself in splendor, without spot or wrinkle or anything like that, but holy and blameless"* (Eph. 5:25-27). Christ looks at the church the way a groom looks at his bride as she walks down the aisle. He is committed to doing everything within his power to ensure she is holy and blameless in every way. Paul also declared, *"Now to him who is able to do above and beyond all that we ask or think according to the power that works in us—to him be glory in the church and in Christ Jesus to all generations, forever and ever. Amen"* (Eph. 3:20-21). How awesome to belong to something Christ loves so much!

Unfortunately, the church often doesn't function the way Christ intended. Currently, 70% of churches in America are plateaued or declining. Many have been scandalized by immorality or disunity. Most aren't living out Ephesians 3:20-21. Numerous congregations have become like the Jerusalemites in Nehemiah's day. They have lived among ruins and rubble for so long it's all they know. Rather than addressing the burned gates and broken walls, they simply inhabit the debris and assume things can never change. That attitude breaks Christ's heart.

If your church is currently seeking its next pastor, you stand at a crossroads. How you handle the situation will determine your church's future. Do you want more of the same, or do you suspect God has far more for your church than you have previously experienced?

Most Christians fail to understand that God's ways are not their ways (Is. 55:8-9). When they do God's work the world's way, the results are dissatisfying. The process of calling a pastor is one example. Well-intentioned churches place their most trusted members on the search committee. They may start and end their meetings with prayer. But far too often, they operate just like a secular organization. At the end of the day, they settle for far less than God intended.

This guide was written to help you seek your church's next pastor. It outlines the major steps involved in the process, warns of common pitfalls, and offers suggestions for ways to protect and bless your church. It doesn't spell out hard-and-fast rules. Each church is unique, and you must seek God's guidance for your situation. But certain challenges are common to most churches, and this guide can help you successfully navigate them.

CHAPTER ONE

Crucial Considerations

M any thoughts may race through your mind when you are selected to serve on a pastor search committee. Am I qualified? How long will it take? How hard will it be? Will we make a cohesive team? What process will we follow?

As you begin the important work of selecting your church's next pastor, keep these truths at the forefront of your mind.

I. The church isn't *yours!*

People often speak about the church as if it belongs to them. They know they don't really own it, but they often *act* as if they do.

Settle this issue at the outset. The church may have started in your living room. You might be a deacon or the longest active member. Perhaps you donated the land on which the building sits. Nevertheless, if you treat the church as yours, you will cause tremendous damage. You can attend it, serve in it, give to it, and pray for it, but you can't give it life, dispense God's blessing to it, or add to it (Matt. 16:18; 1 Cor. 12:18). Only Christ can do that.

Search committee members must release their plans and agendas to Christ and acknowledge that they are merely stewards of his church. If you can't genuinely relinquish your desires, then you will cause more harm than good. Your church doesn't need your best; it needs God's best.

II. Your pastor is not the head of your church!

Too many churches believe God's work grinds to a halt when the pastor leaves. But the risen Christ is the permanent head of your church, and the members are its body. As long as the head and body are in place, a church can do anything!

Unfortunately, pastors often act as if they are the COH (Chief Operating Head) of the church. They may understand that Christ is in charge, yet they behave as if they are the "practical" head. Don't be deceived. There is nothing more practical than having Christ as the head of your church.

Sidenote: When interviewing a pastoral candidate, ask him what member of the body he is (1 Cor. 12). Some pastors covet the "head" position even though they know it belongs to Christ.

III. Getting the wrong pastor can set your church back for years.

Hiring the wrong person could harm your church for years to come. Church history is littered with tragic examples of pastors who left their flock in shambles when they departed. Consider the following examples.

- God led a congregation to plant new churches all over its region. Eventually, the pastor was called to a new assignment. His successor worried his flock wasn't doing enough to care for their own needs. So the church ceased its mission work, and God stopped blessing it. People began arguing about money and leaving. Once the church began trying to "save itself," it could no longer pay its bills or its pastor (Matt. 16:25).

- A long-term pastor eventually retired. He had served the church for forty years and was dearly loved by his congregation and the local community. The next pastor felt threatened by his predecessor's success, so he dismantled every program the previous leader had initiated. He looked askance at church members who remained loyal to the retired minister. Eventually, the church ended up in debt, disarray, and decline.

- A vibrant church was excited about its dynamic new pastor. He was an excellent preacher with a compelling vision for the church. Everything started off great. Then news broke that the pastor was engaged in multiple adulterous affairs. Worse yet, it came to light that he left his former flock due to fallout over his ongoing sexual escapades. The church was devastated and deeply divided as members argued about what to do.

- A church was excited about their pastor's bold goals. A visionary, he immediately launched the congregation into a massive building campaign. But he soon grew angry at those who tried to hold him accountable. As a result of poor business decisions and overextending the debt load, the church couldn't meet its payments and faced foreclosure. At that point, the pastor felt the Lord leading him to begin an itinerant preaching ministry and left the church.

We could fill many pages recording the damage poorly chosen leaders have inflicted on Christ's church. Act wisely and under the Lord's leadership as you undertake the important task of selecting a pastor.

IV. You are NOT in a hurry.

Some church members will want you to make a decision as quickly as possible. They may feel as if the church is dead in the water without a minister at the helm. But calling a pastor shouldn't be a rushed decision. Spend adequate time praying and waiting for God's answer.

To satisfy the church's need for progress without compromising the procedure, take the following steps. First, meet as soon as the committee is named. Second, appoint a chair who will address issues in a timely matter. Third, put an interim plan in place so people are less concerned about day-to-day operations. An interim minister can grant stability while the church seeks a full-time pastor. I know of one congregation that hired a retired school principal to manage church programming during the search process. He enlisted speakers to preach on Sundays and administered the church office and various ministries. He shunned the limelight, but he was diligent and had great people skills. When he began his role, the church drew 250 attendees on Sundays. When the congregation welcomed a new pastor, it averaged 450 people at services and was healthier than ever.

You ought to be determined in your work, but don't panic. The head of your church can accomplish much good during the interim period.

V. Christ loves your church and knows who is best for it.

Christ knows your church better than you do. You might want to hire a new pastor immediately, but God sees the bigger picture. Your church may need to address some issues first. Perhaps the perfect pastor will not be available for six months. An interim minister might bring needed healing to your congregation in preparation for the next pastor's leadership. Trust that Christ loves your church and knows what is best for it.

Part of trusting God is honoring his timing. Rushing ahead of God's schedule is costly (1 Sam. 13). I have known godly men and women who longed for a spouse.

They prayed and waited, but heaven remained silent. Eventually, they panicked and married someone they knew wasn't intended for them. In one case, a bride realized her mistake on her honeymoon and filed for divorce as soon as she returned home. Many of those people learned the hard way that it is better to be alone than to choose the wrong person. It's the same for churches.

Some churches believe they are too small to attract a "good" pastor, so they lower their standards and hire whoever is willing to accept the job. Tragically, those ministers often lead poorly and leave their flock in worse shape than they found it. Quality pastors are not put off by a church's size. They tend to look for potential and people of faith. Henry Blackaby accepted a call to a church of ten people. Great leaders are attracted to great possibilities. Never lower your standards because you assume God doesn't love you enough to give you his best!

VI. Don't use the world's ways to do God's work.

God's activity requires God's methods. Churches often place prominent businesspeople on the pastor search committee. This practice isn't inherently bad. But businesspeople often carry their business practices into the church. Perhaps they are accustomed to enlisting a headhunter to search databases for job candidates, so they presume they can simply farm out the responsibility of finding a pastor to a professional agency. They might decide to hire the person with the most impressive resume. Maybe they call the most dynamic preacher rather than someone with a godly character.

God's ways are not our ways (Is. 55:8-9). Conventional business practices don't always transfer well to the church, but people who have experienced worldly success often struggle to overcome their bias for secular methods. Unsurprisingly, many of today's pastors and worship leaders look more like rock stars than servants of God. Countless worship services have impressive lighting but few transformed lives. The world can fill premises (just look at Disney World), but it cannot set people free from sin.

As a committee, take time to examine your approach. Is it biblical? Is it God-honoring? Does it force you to rely on God or a consultant?

VII. Address issues in your church before hiring your next pastor.

Some pastors leave their flock in great shape when they resign. They lead well and address problems promptly. When they finish, their church is ready to move forward under new leadership.

Other pastors ignore nagging issues. Perhaps a beloved minister served into his 70s. Church members love him like a father, but they also recognize that he neglected major issues. They would be wise not to locate a successor immediately. God may lead them to get their house in order first. Perhaps the aging worship leader needs to move on, but the senior pastor didn't have the heart to let go of his long-time friend. Or perhaps the youth pastor owns a side business and is putting more time and effort into that endeavor than into youth ministry. People have complained about the poorly run youth program for two years, and some families have left the church. The retiring pastor knew there were problems but was concerned that the youth pastor and his wife recently had their first child and needed the income.

Leaving these issues unresolved for the next pastor is unfair. Many ministers arrive at a new post only to discover the previous leader had been too timid to address chronic problems. No pastor wants to begin his tenure by confronting issues that should have been settled before he arrived.

Sometimes financial concerns need to be handled. There may be blatant sin in the congregation that should be confronted. A congregation may have mistreated its former pastor or dismissed him without cause. If church members want God's approval in the future, they must repent of their sinful actions so they are prepared for God to bless them under their next leader.

Ask God if there is any unfinished business that needs to be resolved before you call your next pastor.

VIII. Prepare your church to hear from God.

Churches are often unprepared to hear from God. Consequently, voting for the next pastor is nothing more than a popularity contest. Use the interim period to prepare people to seek God's mind on this crucial matter.

Many churches have used the interim period to launch a church-wide study of *Experiencing God* or *When God Speaks*. God not only prepared the church to make an important decision but also began a fresh work of revival in the congregation.

Don't waste the time between pastors! It offers a wonderful opportunity to ready people for what God has in store.

IX. Eternity is at stake.

The wrong pastor can decimate a church. Teenagers who grow up in a divided congregation may leave the faith. Hurting marriages might end in divorce rather than healing. Prodigal children may never return. Mission opportunities will be lost.

Realize the grave reality of what is at stake. God intends for your church to be a spiritual lighthouse in your community. He expects your church to reach its own children and teenagers for Christ. Many eternal destinies hinge on your church being all God intends for it to be.

Conclusion

Being selected to serve on a pastor search committee is an honor. It indicates your fellow church members trust you to hear from God and act with integrity. Be sure your walk with God is closer than it has ever been. Set aside additional time to hear from God and to immerse yourself in his word. Carefully consider the issues laid before you in this chapter. Then proceed to the important matters that lie ahead.

CHAPTER TWO

Establishing a Search Committee

An important step in finding your church's next pastor is establishing the search committee. It's tempting to use the world's methods to do God's work. But God's ways are not our ways. Each congregation is unique, and churches must seek God's will for their situation. Following these practical guidelines will help you assemble a search committee that is both godly and effective.

I. Who should be considered for the committee?

A. *People of prayer and faith*

Pastor search committee members must know how to recognize God's leading. They need not be top businesspeople. A better fit might be a widow who prays without ceasing. The key is not professional acumen but spiritual sensitivity. Deep faith and a vibrant prayer life should be the minimum threshold for committee members.

B. People without an agenda

Church members may have an agenda for the new pastor. Some might desire change, while others want things to remain as they are. Perhaps certain people long for a more robust senior adult ministry, whereas others would prefer a pastor who invests in young families. Having preferences isn't inherently wrong, but committee members should be able to set their biases aside and seek God's will for their church.

C. Godly people with management or hiring experience

Simply being a successful businessperson is an insufficient reason to serve on a pastor search committee, but having a business or management background is useful.

Some churches choose the godliest prayer warriors to serve on the pastor search committee, but none of the people they select has ever served in management. They may never have reviewed a resume, checked references, or conducted an interview. They might not know how to ask difficult questions, recognize red flags, or maintain control of the discussion. Consequently, well-meaning committees staffed with the saintliest, kindest people from the congregation often make catastrophic mistakes during the hiring process.

It's dangerous to construct a search committee that doesn't have any true leaders on it. A good practice is to include at least one person who is accustomed to conducting job interviews and knows how to evaluate resumes. This person ought to meet the spiritual requirements as well.

D. Someone who has been to seminary or ministered successfully previously or currently

It's helpful if at least one committee member is familiar with ministerial training and staffing issues. Don't include anyone who is actively looking for a ministry job, as a conflict of interest will be inevitable. But someone who has attended seminary or understands ministry dynamics is invaluable to a search committee. Perhaps a church member attended seminary and served on staff at a church before starting her own counselling ministry. She might make an excellent addition to the committee.

This subject will be explored at length in a later chapter, but ministerial resumes can be confusing. Most people are unfamiliar with the difference between Master of Theology, Master of Divinity, and Master of Fine Arts degrees. They may not be able to distinguish between Doctor of Philosophy and Doctor of Ministry degrees. Often, committees are simply happy the candidate attended seminary. But what is the difference between attending a school and earning a degree? What differentiates a Bible college from a Christian university or a seminary? Not all schools are the same. Some are theologically conservative and others are liberal. Some are militantly a certain theological position and others are charismatic. It's important to understand what the applicant's alma mater emphasizes. The candidate may not hold strictly to those views, but the information can direct the line of questioning during the interview process.

Beyond the sphere of education, a variety of terms are used for ministry positions in churches and Christian organizations. It's helpful if someone on your committee understands what they mean. Some terms sound impressive but involve minimal responsibility. Perhaps a resume indicates the candidate took three years to complete an internship that should have required only one. If no one on your committee has ministry experience, you may inadvertently overlook important issues.

Diligent search committees clarify each of these distinctions. If no one on the committee has ministry training or experience, then it's wise to discuss these matters with an outside consultant who can provide insight.

E. People the congregation trusts

Committee members ought to be trustworthy and truly desire God's will for their church. They should also be discreet. Inevitably, people will ask for updates and desire inside information. Committee members must be able to keep their work confidential.

II. Who doesn't automatically qualify to serve on the committee?

Serving on a pastor search committee is one of the most important responsibilities in the church. Committee members should be chosen not for their prestige, attendance records, or popularity but because they are suited for this vital servant role. Sometimes people presume certain church members will be placed on the committee. But heed the following cautions about people who should not automatically be selected for this role.

A. Long-time members

People often assume long-time church members deserve to serve on the pastor search committee. But the church doesn't belong to its charter members. Qualifying to serve on the committee involves more than cumulative years of attendance. Candidates must also meet the spiritual requirements. Selecting committee members based on the length of their membership sets the bar too low.

B. Former committee members

When forming a committee, churches tend to return to the same people each time. They may be viewed as the godliest or most influential members of the congregation, but they should have greater qualifications than simply having served on past committees. People ought to re-qualify each time a committee is established.

A church may need to form a search committee multiple times in a brief period due to pastors' short tenures. The church might be quick to re-enlist the same people for each committee. But if each pastor the committee selects leaves within a year or two, the committee's process may be flawed. Choosing new members might encourage a more God-centered approach. People's schedules and availability also change. It's preferable to take a fresh look each time for those who are currently best suited to serve.

C. Wealthy members

Just because people are wealthy or make substantial donations doesn't mean they are qualified to serve in this important role. Large donors may assume they will have a major voice in selecting the next pastor, but no one owns the church. Giving sizeable financial donations doesn't grant a person greater spiritual authority in a congregation. Committee members must be people of faith and prayer. Being wealthy or generous shouldn't disqualify someone from serving, but having the necessary spiritual qualifications is crucial.

D. Deacons, church administrators

A church's bylaws may demand that at least one member of the deacon or elder board serve on the pastor search committee. This practice is typically used as a safeguard to ensure the committee fulfills its purpose. But selecting unspiritual people for a role merely because of the office they hold compromises the spiritual integrity of the entire committee. Presumably, deacons should be known for their piety, prayer life, and faith. But if the only reason someone is placed on the committee is because of his position in the church, then that appointment ought to be reconsidered.

E. Church staff

Placing staff members on the search committee is unwise, because it is difficult for them to separate their role and concerns from those of the broader church. For example, the search committee might interview someone who holds staff to high standards of accountability. This practice may be great for the church but intimidating to a staff person. While there are exceptions, it is wiser to consult with staff without making them committee members.

F. Someone who would like to apply for the position

If someone would like to be considered for the senior pastor role, he should not serve on the committee. Human nature tends to abuse positions of influence for personal gain. For example, perhaps Bill is seeking a new ministry job after returning from the mission field due to his son's illness. If the church selects him to serve on the committee because of his missions experience, he may inadvertently convince other committee members to choose him for the role. Far too often, well-meaning search committees act kindly toward an unemployed minister rather than prayerfully seeking God's will for their church. Bill should be asked directly if he is interested in the position. If so, he should submit a resume and refrain from serving on the committee.

G. Someone who is too busy to attend meetings

Some church members are wonderful Christians but have little time to serve on a committee. The congregation may feel remiss in not enlisting trusted church members. But committees are compromised when its members are unable to give the work adequate attention. If people cannot regularly attend meetings, they should not be placed on the committee.

III. Size and composition of the committee.

There is not a universally right or wrong way to compose a pastor search committee. Church bylaws may lay out certain guidelines. The following recommendations come from years of experience.

A. Between 5-7 members

The exact number of committee members may vary from church to church. The key is efficiency. A committee with too many members will struggle to find times when everyone is available to meet. Committees of 5-7 people are ideal, because they are large enough to allow members to miss meetings occasionally but small enough to be easily managed.

B. Not necessarily representative of every demographic

Some churches like to include people from various demographics on the committee. They may select a senior adult, a middle-aged adult, a single adult, a person from the ethnic church plant, a youth, etc. While this configuration appears inclusive, it can also be as unwieldy as a joint session of Congress. Better to keep the numbers small and choose members carefully so people from all demographics find them trustworthy.

C. Include both men and women

Search committees should include both male and female members. Men and women see and hear things differently. Women may be more perceptive of how the pastor treats his wife, children, and other women. Committees that don't include representatives from each gender will almost certainly have blind spots.

D. Elect a chair during the first meeting

A chair should be selected soon after the committee is formed. Some church bylaws may designate who this person should be. If not, the committee ought to choose someone who is respected and recognized for having leadership ability. No committee member should seek or campaign for the position (such a person should not be on the committee in the first place). Ideally, the chair will also have good public speaking skills and be able to gain the congregation's trust.

IV. Determining eligibility

In many congregational churches, the membership at large selects committee members. Therefore, eligibility is an important issue.

Most churches allow only members to serve on the committee. Other congregations restrict eligibility even further. For example, though a church might baptize and grant membership to five-year-olds, youth may not qualify to serve on the committee until they are sixteen or eighteen years old.

Another possible restriction pertains to inactive members. Church rolls typically include many people who no longer attend services. Perhaps some members have moved out of the area. Others may have stopped going to church altogether. In either case, letting lapsed members serve on the committee is inappropriate.

A final consideration regarding eligibility concerns active church members who have moral, spiritual, or other issues that bar them from service. Perhaps a well-known member is experiencing marital difficulties. The deacons might be aware of this issue and know it is unwise for him to attend weekly meetings. Or perhaps a member has created much conflict in the congregation, doesn't support the church financially, or holds heretical theological views. The deacons, elders, or staff may determine not to allow the person to serve on such a sensitive committee.

V. Selecting members

Electing committee members may be handled in one of at least four ways. The first and most straightforward method is for the church to list the names of all adult church members and trust the congregation to vote for those they most respect as spiritual leaders.

A second approach is for a deacon or elder board to purge the member list of anyone they consider to be ineligible for the role and then allow the congregation to vote on those who remain. This process typically prevents unqualified people from being selected.

A third method requires the board of deacons or elders to approve the final list of people the church body elects. The congregation votes on the candidates they prefer, but the board can veto a nomination if they believe the person's participation could harm the process.

A fourth approach is for the deacon body or elder board to present a list of 5-7 names to the congregation for a vote of affirmation.

Churches have used all of these methods effectively. Choose one that works within your church structure.

VI. Commissioning prayer

Once committee members have been selected, formally pray over them. Invite them to stand at the front of the auditorium while select people offer a focused prayer on their behalf. The congregation might surround them and offer silent prayer. This special time will bless the committee members and remind the congregation to pray for the committee regularly in the days ahead.

Conclusion

Properly composing a committee is crucial to its effectiveness. The process should not be based on people's feelings but on what is most God-honoring. A search committee's task is too important to entrust to a carelessly assembled team.

CHAPTER THREE

Setting the Ground Rules

In God's eyes, how you do something is as important as what you do. Establish certain procedures at the outset to guide how your committee functions. Doing so can prevent complications from arising later in the process.

I. Prayer

Some committee members may be anxious to begin discussing issues and possible candidates right away, but don't forget that prayer is a vital part of the process. After selecting a chair, it's wise to devote the first month of meetings to prayer.

First, get into position to hear from God together. Committee members will undoubtedly come from various walks of life and have diverse perspectives, experiences, and concerns. Developing unity of heart and mind takes time. But if you honestly lift your concerns before God each week, the Holy Spirit will bring you into harmony with each other so you can hear from God together. Focusing your prayer on who God is rather than on what you want will transform the process from the beginning.

Second, allow God to open your understanding to what matters. You may start out with a list of priorities. But as you pray, God will reveal what he knows is significant. Don't make critical decisions before the Holy Spirit has granted you wisdom.

Third, give the congregation time to pray. Part of your role is to prepare the congregation for its next pastor. If you hastily obtain a candidate, the congregation may not yet recognize God's provision. Don't move forward until the candidate, church body, and committee are in alignment with God's will.

II. Confidentiality

Your work ought to be confidential. Certain information may be shared with the congregation if appropriate, but use discretion when disclosing details about a candidate. The search process can become divisive when rumors start swirling. Committee members who reveal sensitive information should be reprimanded. If they continue to break confidentiality, they ought to be removed from the committee. Integrity and trustworthiness are non-negotiables. Consider having each committee member sign a covenant document at the outset promising to maintain confidentiality.

III. Unanimity

Address the issue of unanimity early on. Some committees function on the basis of majority vote, while others proceed only if the vote is unanimous. Requiring unanimity may seem cumbersome, as it essentially gives each member veto power. But it also makes unity essential in all your committee does. Reaching a harmonious decision is possible only when each member puts aside personal desires and seeks the Lord's will through prayer.

IV. Respect

Committee members must show respect for the chair, each other, and the congregation. Disrespectful behavior has no place on a committee that is earnestly seeking God's direction. Ephesians 4:29 could be a great guiding verse for your discussions.

V. Efficient use of time

Committee members are busy people, so don't squander time. Meetings ought to begin and end punctually. The chair should produce an agenda for each meeting and facilitate the discussion, intervening if someone is monopolizing the conversation or when it's time to move on to the next matter of business.

VI. Meetings

Committees should meet regularly in the beginning, preferably weekly. Doing so provides ample time for prayer. If finding the next pastor takes longer than a few months, meeting less often may be prudent. Throughout the process, frequently communicate your progress with the church body. The congregation will want to know that you are diligently seeking the pastor God has for their church.

VII. Reserve members

Some churches elect two to three reserve committee members. One church elected eight committee members and three alternates. The eight people who received the most votes were the active members, and the three people with the next highest vote totals became alternates. The committee decided to allow the alternates to attend meetings as non-voting members so they would be up to speed if they were called on to serve. The alternates became intimately involved in the process and were soon treated as regular members.

Typically, the best practice is to elect a committee large enough to sustain the normal loss of one or two members or to enlist additional members only if the need arises.

Conclusion

This chapter doesn't cover every issue your committee must address at the outset, but it includes some of the most common ones. When in doubt about how to proceed, pray and allow God to guide you with his wisdom. If you begin well, you are in a better position to end well.

CHAPTER FOUR

Getting Started

With the committee in place and the ground rules established, it's time to move on to the important job of finding your church's next leader. One of your first tasks is to determine what process you will use to find candidates.

I. Find Candidates

A. Enlist a personnel services agency

Churches sometimes use an agency to locate and vet candidates. Agencies have large databases of potential applicants. After narrowing the search based on the criteria you provide, the agency will present a list of names and help direct the interview process. These agencies typically have the means to investigate candidates in ways most churches can't.

While this approach is becoming popular, it has drawbacks. The agency is a business seeking to make a profit. It may be a Christian organization, but it doesn't have the same interest in the outcome that you have. Its vetting processes aren't failproof. Some red flags may be overlooked through normal investigative channels. Agencies also have a natural interest in finishing the job as quickly as possible. While these services may be effective, most churches take the search process on themselves.

B. Broadcast the position

Another common method of finding candidates is to advertise the position widely online and in other public venues. The advantage of this approach is that it quickly reaches a large audience. The downside is that many people are looking for a ministry job! You will likely be inundated with applications, and the process of sifting through resumes is time consuming and often fruitless.

This traditional means of "getting the word out" is rarely productive, because most respondents fall into one of two categories: either they are unemployed or they have a job but want a better one. Neither situation is promising.

If a pastor is unemployed, find out why. Many people who apply for senior pastor posts have been unable to obtain or maintain a ministry position previously. If twelve other churches turned a candidate down, you might question why you are considering him. He may be a diamond in the rough. More likely, you will learn why a dozen other churches didn't hire him.

Likewise, be wary if a candidate is actively searching for a better job. L. R. Scarborough, second president of Southwestern Baptist Theological Seminary, once observed, "If your place is not great enough to suit you, make it so. The minister who is unable to make a place great is too weak to hold a great one." It's better to find a minister who is happily growing a church than to hire someone who is chronically dissatisfied and ineffective.

For these reasons and more, be cautious about advertising too widely.

C. Use denominational channels

If your church belongs to a denomination, searching within your denomination narrows the candidate pool to people who hold similar theological viewpoints. Denominational leaders should be able alert you if a pastor has experienced problems in other churches in the past. Sadly, some leaders are careless in their recommendations. They may feel badly for a pastor who was dismissed from his previous two assignments or try to help a friend get a new position. Conduct a thorough investigation into each candidate regardless of how highly recommended he comes.

While denominational channels can be a helpful resource, keep in mind that the pastor God has in mind for your church might not currently be serving in your denomination.

D. Use resources God has made available

The Lord may have already provided connections to a new pastor if you pay attention. Perhaps the ideal candidate currently works at your church in another capacity. Maybe the youth pastor or an associate pastor has served effectively and is ready for greater responsibility. One of the first places you ought to look is within your church's sphere of influence. This approach is effective for a few reasons. First, your committee already knows the person and is less likely to be unpleasantly surprised. Second, staff are familiar with the church's culture and mission, which will make the transition smoother. Finally, moving costs will be negligible.

One church had an outstanding pastor. When he left, several members believed the associate would make a perfect replacement. Everyone liked him, and he knew and supported the church culture. But some members argued that it would be easier to replace the senior pastor than to find another associate pastor as effective as the one they had. They ultimately hired an inferior senior pastor and lost their associate to another church.

Sometimes God connects people with your church in other ways. Someone might comment, "I know a person who would make a fantastic pastor, but I can't imagine him ever leaving his current ministry position." Pursue that person as a candidate. God may be working in his heart in ways others can't yet see.

II. Things NOT to do!

Some standard operating procedures pastor search committees practice, though common, are inadvisable.

A. Survey the church for its preferences

Pastor search manuals often suggest commencing the process by surveying church members about what they want in the next pastor. The committee then tabulates the data and builds a profile based on the results. This process engages the congregation and lets them know the committee is taking their concerns into account.

Though this practice may seem sensible, it has several flaws. First, as Henry Blackaby has often said, "If you ask the wrong question, you'll get the wrong answer." Don't ask, "What would you like in a pastor?" Ask instead, "After prayer and Bible study, what type of pastor do you believe God wants for our church?" The first question is self-centered; the second is God-centered.

Second, finding someone who perfectly matches everyone's wishes is impossible. People may be disappointed that the candidate who is eventually proposed has only three of the six qualities they requested. Engaging in anything that will inevitably disappoint people is unwise!

Third, pastors aren't perfect. Rarely do they embody every good quality people desire, yet God can still use them powerfully. One church surveyed the congregation to learn what they wanted in a pastor. The profile they developed indicated that the pastor should be 45, have two teenage children (one boy and one girl), have twenty years of experience, and demonstrate a passion for evangelism. The church looked far and wide but couldn't find a candidate who met that criteria.

Eventually, they noticed a young man who didn't fit the profile. He was a Ph.D. student who had never held a church job. He had two preschool boys, no teenagers or daughters. While he sought to evangelize, his leadership style leaned far more toward discipleship. Though this young man didn't have any of the distinctive qualities the survey had highlighted, the church began discussions with him anyway. They ultimately called him to be their pastor, and God began working in the church. Young families and college students started attending and joining. A sweet spirit developed. Eventually, the church became a top leader in its denomination for baptisms and giving. Many claimed those were that church's best years, and they happened under a pastor who scored 0% on the congregational survey! Sometimes our desires and God's agenda are misaligned. It's always better to go with God's will.

Fourth, church members don't always know what they need. They may not have a clue what God intends to do in their church. They don't know whether the economy will skyrocket or plummet. They can't predict that an ethnic population will begin moving into their neighborhood in large numbers. Church members also make faulty assumptions. If the church has numerous senior citizens, the congregation may believe they need a pastor in his sixties. A better fit may be a 40-year-old minister who loves seniors and delights in making home and hospital visits. Perhaps a church wants to reach young families, so they profile a pastor in his late twenties or early thirties. Yet God may have chosen a 55-year-old pastor with a background in marital counselling who can become a mentor and guide to many young couples. The key is not for the pastor to be the same age as the target demographic but to find a leader with a passion and skill set to meet the church's needs.

B. Hire someone who is the opposite of the last pastor

People often advise pastor search committees to hire someone who is the opposite of the previous minister. The rationale is simple. If a church had an evangelistic pastor for the last 15 years, it should hire someone skilled in discipleship who can properly minister to the new converts. Or perhaps the previous pastor was a visionary who started many new programs and greatly expanded the facilities. The next pastor must be good at administration and raising funds to pay for everything his predecessor commenced.

This reasoning makes sense at a surface level, but it is faulty. I will offer one caveat here: If the last minister was a failure, then change is in order. But if the previous pastor was effective, it may be unwise to choose a replacement who is his polar opposite.

If a visionary pastor led successfully for fifteen years, many people resonated with his ministry style. He likely hired staff who synced well with him. Church programing supports his methods. Some change may be in order, but a pastor who ministers in a completely different way won't connect with the vast majority of church members.

We know of one church that had a pastor for 12 years who encouraged the congregation to plant churches and do mission work. The Lord always provided. When that beloved minister left, the church hired a pastor to shore up the base and help the church develop stronger financial reserves. The new pastor didn't start church plants, and he disbanded some of the existing ones. Business meetings sounded more like a report from the annual auditor than a time to share exciting accounts of God's activity. Donations dried up because there were no longer steps of faith to support. The new pastor seemed inclined to walk by sight rather than by faith. Attendance and finances plummeted. Cost-cutting measures were implemented. Staff members were released. Programs were discontinued. The only thing the new pastor was known for was what he shut down. The contrast between the two pastors couldn't have been starker, and the results were devastating.

Churches, like people, have personalities. They have strengths and weaknesses. While it's noble to seek to balance out your church's weaknesses, it is also wise to play to its strengths. In time, God may shift your church to a more balanced approach. Be cautious of lurching back and forth with each new minister. If God has given you several pastors with a similar ministry style, you probably have a church full of people who are responsive to that approach.

C. Hiring someone just like the previous pastor

While automatically hiring someone who is the exact opposite of your last pastor is unwise, it's also imprudent to hunt high and low for his replica. Every pastor has weaknesses, and he is probably keenly aware of them. The key is to find someone who supports the previous minister's work while gently introducing new strengths.

Perhaps the former leader was a whirlwind of activity who was always stirring things up and leaving his staff to organize the mess. Everyone loved him, so they accommodated his idiosyncrasies. But the next minister, while fully supportive of the ministries his predecessor launched, might be better at encouraging the staff. Perhaps they breathe a sigh of relief when the new senior pastor listens to their concerns and finds ways to obtain the resources they need for their work. Or perhaps the former minister was a builder who doubled the physical footprint of the church and left it in debt. The new pastor can praise his predecessor's accomplishments and vision and perhaps launch a fundraising campaign to pay off the buildings. Rather than diminishing the former leader's contributions, his successor can affirm him and undergird his work.

D. Not having a protocol for handling feedback and unsolicited suggestions

A search committee rarely lacks input from people both within and outside the church. People may want to "bend the ear" of a committee member to express concerns or recommend an approach.

As a general rule, you ought to be prepared to receive counsel and suggestions. Being perceived as aloof and unapproachable can worry the congregation. But conducting one-on-one meetings with people about the search process is dangerous. It's better to encourage people to submit suggestions to the committee as a whole.

Your committee ought to follow the procedures you have established and not succumb to outside pressures. At times, you may need to respond, "We have looked at your suggestions, but we feel led to continue on the path (or schedule) we have already determined."

Stand together as a committee when outside voices make demands. Once you have prayerfully identified the approach God wants you to take, don't waver from it. Be open to good advice, but respond as a committee, not as individuals.

Conclusion

Many issues can arise through the course of committee work. This manual cannot anticipate all of them. Seek the Lord, stay unified, and enlist counsel when necessary. Then process each situation together. The Lord loves your church, and he will guide you if you let him.

CHAPTER FIVE

Setting a Profile

Early in the search process, consider what type of pastor your church needs. A previous chapter examined the popular practice of surveying the church body and deemed it unwise. Some churches essentially announce the job vacancy and then hire the most talented applicant. This strategy has some merit. But just because a pastor is highly gifted does not necessarily mean he is the right fit for your congregation. It behooves you to reflect on your church's specific needs.

I. Use biblical guidelines

A first step for every committee is to review biblical qualifications for pastors. 1 Timothy 3:1-7 is a good starting place.

v. 2. An overseer, therefore, must be above reproach

Above reproach doesn't mean perfect or sinless. It suggests that after the pastor has sinned, he has acknowledged his error, repented of it, turned from his wicked ways, and lived in a God-honoring manner henceforth. Being "above reproach" means people can't point to something in a person's life that continues to cause concern.

Some people have a cloud hanging over them. A minister may have been accused of sexual or financial misconduct. Being above reproach might mean he submitted himself fully to investigation and was found innocent. On the other hand, perhaps someone has been accused of the same offense repeatedly. While he might not have been proven guilty, he may trigger enough red flags that a search committee is wise to bypass him at that time.

The husband of one wife

There has been much debate about what this qualification entails. First, though scripture certainly upholds women as people of godly influence in the church, this passage implies the senior pastor is a man. The Greek phrase literally means "a one-woman man." This verse has traditionally been understood to exclude men who were divorced and remarried from serving as a pastor, since they had two wives. But this interpretation is problematic. For one, it also bars widowers who remarry and single men from the pastoral office (which may have disqualified the apostle Paul who wrote this statement!). The Greek language had a word for divorce. If Paul wanted to prohibit divorced people from serving as pastors, he could have just said so.

It's more prudent to take the first two phrases together. The senior pastor ought to be wholly committed to his wife *if* he has one, and he should be above reproach in how he treats her. A person may become divorced for many reasons. Some godly men have discovered that their wife was committing adultery. The wife then sued for divorce despite everything her husband did to save the marriage. Of course, no spouse is perfect. Perhaps the pastor neglected his wife at times out of a misguided zeal to serve the Lord in the church or failed to take her concerns seriously enough. How the pastor conducted himself in his marriage and through the divorce must be considered when determining if he is above reproach. He may not be guilty of adultery, but his behavior during and after the fact could reveal that he is unprepared to step into another ministerial role.

There are also tragic cases in which the minister is responsible for the divorce. Perhaps he committed adultery and left his wife. Sometimes these former pastors ultimately marry their mistress. After an "appropriate" period away, they may profess that God has forgiven them and they sense a freedom to re-enter the ministry.

This scenario is much more troubling. A pastor committing adultery is a heinous offense that greatly dishonors his Lord. He knew what God's word says on the matter, yet he gave way to his carnal passions anyway. Adultery is a character sin. It involves breaking vows he made before God and witnesses, despite the grievous harm it causes his spouse, children, and church. It doesn't happen merely in an indiscreet moment. It demonstrates a lack of integrity that a simple apology or a brief period out of the ministry cannot overcome.

Being "above reproach" makes re-entry into a church leadership position extremely difficult after committing adultery. God will certainly forgive someone who genuinely repents of his sin. But if a person was unfaithful to his wife while serving as a pastor, he will always carry that failing with him. Those looking for an excuse for their own infidelity can point to the pastor and claim, "Even the pastor has done it!" This reasoning may seem unfair, but it underscores why pastors must be above reproach.

A final issue related to divorce concerns people who divorced before becoming Christians. For instance, one man was married as a young adult and living a party lifestyle. He was radically saved and began to live fully for Christ. His transformation offended his non-Christian wife who hadn't signed up to be married to a "Jesus freak," so she divorced him. He later felt called into ministry and married a godly wife. His situation presents different issues. If divorce under all circumstances is a disqualification, then he is ineligible to serve as a pastor. If he were the one who left his wife, he might be barred from ministry. But losing his wife because he was zealous about following Christ is a different scenario altogether. How he handled the situation can speak loudly to whether he is above reproach.

This issue is complex and one your committee should address before examining resumes.

Self-controlled

People often overlook this qualification. But what about grossly overweight pastors? What about ministers who are addicted to TV, video games, or other activities? An obese or short-tempered pastor will have difficulty preaching to others about self-control.

Sensible

Is he wise? Does he give solid counsel? Does he act foolishly in certain areas of his life? Look at the personal and professional decisions he has made thus far to determine how sensible he is.

Respectable

Does he hold his office with honor? Pastors often have a delightful sense of humor. But some ministers lack propriety. They may act foolishly in public. Others are careless with their dress or grooming. Some are poor managers of their money or property. They may be unaware that the thoughtless way they manage themselves loses people's respect. In a society that has little regard for professional pastors, churches can't afford to hire a minister who invites criticism by his sloppy hygiene or poor people skills. Pastors ought to gain favor from people in the community, government, and local businesses by the way they conduct themselves. Your pastor is a reflection of your church. Choose someone who will represent you well.

Hospitable

Hospitality was a valued trait in the ancient world. It reflected a pragmatic concern for people's needs. Pastors should be shepherds who genuinely care about their sheep's wellbeing. A minister's hospitality demonstrates that he cares for his flock not only from the pulpit but also from around his kitchen table.

Able to teach

A minister must be able to handle scripture accurately and instruct people in its meaning and application. A pastor's teaching occurs in a classroom, from the pulpit, beside a hospital bed, and in numerous other settings.

It's worth noting that the qualification here is to teach, but a minister should also be a capable preacher. It's difficult to build a church strictly on solid sermons, but it's much more challenging to grow a church without them. Watch videos of the candidate preaching and visit a service to observe him in person. Not everyone is a great speaker, but most people can develop basic preaching skills. Pay attention to the depth of his teaching. How studied and prepared is he? How well does he illustrate his points and apply them to daily living? Some people have a great stage presence but shallow content. Better to have a strong biblical teacher who will feed the congregation spiritual meat each week than to have someone who simply looks good on TV.

v. 3. Not an excessive drinker

The Bible doesn't explicitly forbid alcohol consumption, but it prohibits excess and drunkenness. In cultures in which alcohol has caused enormous pain from addiction, drunk driving, domestic abuse, and violence, it is advisable to follow Paul's advice and refrain from imbibing in anything that may cause others to stumble (1 Cor. 8:13). A church should never feel reluctant to demand that the pastor abstain from alcohol. Having consumed alcohol in the past shouldn't automatically disqualify someone from the job. But if a candidate indulges in frequent alcohol consumption, he may struggle to give it up after accepting the position. If your church desires a pastor who abstains from alcohol, it's probably best to hire someone who already holds those convictions.

Not a bully, but gentle

Pastors should be shepherds, not cattle drivers. They ought to lead their sheep with humility and love. Bullying can occur in numerous ways. Some pastors threaten to resign to get their way. Others may frequently fire staff or dismiss volunteers. They might put people on guilt trips or call them out from the pulpit. Bullies don't know how to love people into following them, so they resort to force. Ask references about their experience working with the candidate. Have the applicant describe his leadership style and how he handles people who disagree with him. Bullies often leave behind tell-tale signs of their bad behavior.

Not quarrelsome

Argumentative people are more concerned with being right than with helping people be set free. A quarrelsome nature reflects a lack of trust in the Holy Spirit's ability to work in people's lives. It may also point to insecurity and an absence of self-control. Wise pastors recognize that they can't argue people into God's kingdom. Confrontational people tend to want to have the last word, but godly leaders present God's Word and trust it to do its appointed work.

Not greedy

People don't typically enter the ministry to become wealthy, but a pastor might be tempted to misuse church funds and resources if he struggles with greed.

Greed is an un-Christlike character trait that is unbecoming of a Christian minister. Some pastors become preoccupied with material concerns to the neglect of their congregation. They may seek to earn additional income, especially if their church is unable to provide adequate financial support. These added responsibilities can take their focus away from their flock. When possible, it's best for a church to pay the pastor a reasonable salary so he can give his full attention to his ministry work.

Be attentive to the financial concerns a candidate expresses during the hiring process. While it's not inherently unspiritual for someone to want to know what his financial compensation will be and whether it will adequately provide for his family, salary shouldn't be the deciding factor in whether he accepts the position. If God is clearly calling him to the church, then he must trust the Lord's provision.

v. 4-5. He must manage his own household competently and have his children under control with all dignity. (If anyone does not know how to manage his own household, how will he take care of God's church?)

While each situation is unique and must be evaluated individually, be wary of hiring a pastor whose children have rejected Christ or are experiencing dramatic struggles, such as a drug addiction or criminal activity. The minister may be a good man but a poor leader. Scripture clearly warns that if a father has been unable to lead his own children to respect him and love God, then he probably won't lead the church well either.

When interviewing a pastoral candidate, ask about his children. If he is defensive of the line of questioning or views your concern as irrelevant, you've uncovered a red flag. A godly pastor will be heartbroken and humbled by a wayward child and should recognize that the church is wise to examine the issue. At times, someone with a prodigal child may prudently refrain from taking a ministry position for a season so he can concentrate on restoring the child to a healthy relationship with his family and with God.

If a pastor neglects to correct ungodly behavior in his offspring, then he is unlikely to address sin in his congregation. If a pastor fails to help his children grow in Christ, he is unlikely to lead his flock to Christian maturity. If his children don't respect him, the church body probably won't either. Scripture indicates that the best way to know what kind of influence a pastor will have on a church is to look at his family.

v. 6. He must not be a new convert

This qualification is prudent for several reasons. First, new converts should focus on their own growth before leading others. Second, the best way to judge a person's character is to evaluate his past behavior. New converts don't have a long track record. They may be zealous, but it's difficult to know if they will persevere through temptation or hardship. Third, spiritual growth can be nurtured but not rushed. Giving new believers major responsibility to guide others may put them beyond their spiritual capacity. Finally, giving new converts great responsibility can foster pride. There are good reasons why the Bible cautions against doing so.

v. 7. He must have a good reputation among outsiders

A pastor represents his church to the outside world. If he is delinquent in paying his debts, loses his temper in public, or behaves badly in any way, he tarnishes his church's witness in the community. A minister's conduct ought to enhance his church's reputation, not diminish it.

These verses comprise just one biblical passage describing the required characteristics for pastors. Take time as a committee to consider what qualities the Bible says a pastor should have. Compile your own list and then incorporate those traits into your profile. Be careful not to adjust or compromise a qualification if you find a candidate who falls short of the Bible's expectations.

II. Prayerfully consider what God has done in the past and what you sense he wants to do in the future.

If your previous pastor's ministry was fruitful, your committee should take time to review what God did during his tenure. Did many young couples become members? Did an ethnic group begin attending in noticeable numbers? Did the youth ministry grow? Did the children's area reach capacity? Even though the previous pastor left, God is still present and desires to continue working. If God added many young families under the last minister, the next pastor may need to lead a building campaign to construct a new children's center. The important thing is not that he has the same personality type as the last leader but that he can build on what God did through his predecessor.

When communicating with candidates, provide a summary of what God has been doing in the church during the past five years. Applicants ought to embrace God's activity. Insecure people who feel threatened by a former pastor's success shouldn't be considered for the role.

III. Develop a profile that is succinct, focused, and flexible.

When developing a profile of what characteristics and qualifications the next pastor should have, don't include every wishful idea your committee conjures. Focus on what matters most. No pastor can do everything. He must meet basic scriptural qualifications. He should also be able to build on the work God did under his predecessor. You may sense that a strong pulpit ministry is important or that he should be capable of undertaking a building program. But be cautious of getting bogged down in how many children you hope he has or whether he follows college football. Allow God room to surprise you with some unique qualities you never even thought to require.

Conclusion

It's wise to consider what type of person is best suited to your ministry. But be aware that God often works through unlikely people. No one would have picked Gideon to lead the Israelites in battle or Moses to free them or any of the twelve disciples to be Jesus' apostles. Ultimately, the key is to be sensitive to the person God knows will be best for your church.

CHAPTER SIX

Communicating with the Congregation

Certain issues can easily divide congregations during the pastor search process. A frequent source of tension is when search committees fail to relay timely information to the church body. People often feel anxious without a pastor, so sharing progress reports can be reassuring. To keep people at ease, communicate information as frequently and fully as possible.

I. Share from the pulpit

A committee member, typically the chair, should give brief updates from the pulpit, perhaps weekly or biweekly. Some committees wait to share a report until they have concrete information to divulge, but your congregation would likely appreciate regular reminders that you are actively seeking God's guidance. The chair might state, "This week the committee met and devoted the entire meeting to prayer. We'll take action soon, but we feel it's crucial to be in sync with God's leading before we move forward." Or a committee member may share, "We are in the process of collecting resumes. For the next month, we'll devote our meetings to prayer as we allow time for interested candidates to apply. In a month, we'll evaluate the resumes and move to the next stage in the process." The congregation deserves to know you are taking your assignment seriously.

II. Report in church business meetings

The committee should share a progress report at every congregational business meeting or church council meeting. Hearing a report or asking a basic question can allay most people's concerns. Answer any questions that don't compromise confidentiality.

III. Request prayer

Asking for prayer broadcasts that you are relying on God's guidance. It also involves the congregation in the process. Seeking a pastor is a valuable teaching tool. You might choose a specific prayer focus each month. Encourage every demographic to pray for their next leader. Speak to the youth about seeking God's provision daily. Explain to the children why they should pray for their pastor. Challenge the senior adults to pray. When the next pastor arrives, everyone will have played an important role in the decision. Hopefully, the church body will continue to pray for the pastor throughout his tenure.

IV. Be careful what you share

Be as transparent as is prudent, but keep some information confidential. For example, it's best not to disclose a candidate's name early in the process for a few reasons. First, his current congregation may be upset if they discover their pastor is considering a new job. Second, the church may be divided if they know several people are being considered. Finally, the candidate may be embarrassed if the committee later decides not to pursue him. Keep names confidential until you are ready to invite a candidate to preach at your church.

Mentioning specific issues the search process uncovers is also unwise. You may be privy to personal and potentially embarrassing information. Handle the situation with grace and discretion.

Conclusion

As a rule, update the congregation as thoroughly and frequently as is judicious. But when in doubt, refrain. Assuaging curiosity is not a compelling reason to disclose confidential information.

CHAPTER 7

Evaluating Candidates

Evaluating resumes and speaking to references isn't glamorous or exciting, but it's a crucial step in the pastor search process. Give this task the thorough, thoughtful treatment it deserves.

I. General issues to consider at the outset

Keep some broad principles in mind as you review resumes. First, recognize that resumes are designed to put candidates in the best light. They inevitably highlight strengths and minimize weaknesses.

Second, note what's missing. Perhaps an applicant lists his extensive education and experience, but careful examination uncovers a three-year break. When pressed about what he had been doing during that time, he may confess he was fired from a church due to personal issues. He didn't list his failure on his resume.

Third, evaluate the resume's professionalism. Many apps and helps are available to make a resume look impressive. If there are typos or if the layout demonstrates little attention to detail, beware! If people are sloppy when applying for a job, how will they handle the position if they obtain it?

II. What to do with unsolicited resumes

Ask these three important questions when examining an unsolicited resume:

A. *Is this person currently employed?* If not, or if he is not serving as a pastor, ask why. There is a big difference between a former international missionary who left the field so his child could receive specialized medical treatment in America and someone who was fired from his previous two jobs.

B. *If this person is serving as a pastor, why does he want to leave his current position?* Some pastors serve in small settings that don't pay a living wage. They may prefer a job that allows them to devote their full attention to serving their church. Others are constantly looking to move to a more robust congregation. Be wary of pastors who see your church as a stepping stone to a still bigger ministry down the road.

C. *Has the candidate submitted resumes to numerous churches?* If someone applies indiscriminately to every vacant church position, he may simply want a job. A pastor should be compensated for his work, but hopefully he views his ministry as more than a means of paying his bills. There is a difference between prayerfully considering a specific position and merely applying to every job opening that comes along.

III. Carefully examine track records

The best indicator of how a pastor will guide your church is how he led his previous congregations. For instance, one search committee interviewed an unemployed minister who had previously served in four churches. The committee asked him why he left each one. He confessed that he was fired from all four positions. A neon red flag! But then he proceeded to explain why he wasn't to blame for any of his dismissals. In one instance, the church patriarchs got angry and fired him when he implemented needed change. He encouraged another church to be more evangelistic, but people resisted his work and let him go. One church became polarized when he sought to start new ministries, so he left rather than divide his flock. He sounded convincing. The committee hired him without digging any deeper into his past. Sadly, that church soon discovered why his previous four congregations asked him to leave and followed suit.

Pay attention to a pastor's track record. It likely offers a glimpse into his future.

Short Tenure

Some pastors never stay more than three years in one position. They may enjoy the "honeymoon" season but not the hard work of leading a church forward. Perhaps they have a limited sermon repertoire and begin looking for a new audience after they have preached through their stock of messages. Whatever the reason, frequently bouncing to new jobs is a red flag.

Growth

Did the candidate's previous churches grow under his leadership? When evaluating a resume, take note if an applicant focuses on the programs he started or stopped rather than on growth. It's concerning if a pastor says he "turned a corner" while leading his last church. That term often means he made a lot of changes, but the church never grew. A leader's job is not to turn corners but to facilitate growth. Some pastors busily attend meetings and make changes while their church attendance steadily declines. In one case, a pastor noted that he had shut down the previous three churches he led. He determined they had reached the end of their life cycle and needed to be given a proper burial. Beware of hiring someone with that particular gifting!

Conflict

Some ministers point to the conflict they perpetually experience as proof of the "spiritual warfare" following them. But even though a conscientious pastor must confront ungodly behavior at times, his ministry shouldn't be characterized by conflict. Instead, a pastor ought to guide his flock with gentleness and love.

Division

Some pastors are polarizing. They tend to see people as either for them or against them. Rather than uniting the church body, they drive wedges between factions. A pastor should be a unifier, not a divider. Frequently experiencing discord could indicate the candidate is a weak leader, lacks sufficient people skills, or has personality issues.

Cooperation with other churches

Does the candidate attend local meetings for pastors? Is he involved with associational or denominational ministries? Avoid calling a minister who doesn't cooperate with others. Be especially wary if a candidate explains that the reason he has been uncooperative is because none of the pastors in his area are godly or orthodox!

Leaving debts

If a pastor leads his church to construct an expensive facility or launch an extensive ministry and then leaves in the critical stages of its development, be cautious. His behavior may reflect a character issue that could be repeated in your church.

Evangelism

How many baptisms did his previous church conduct? Did anyone feel called into ministry under his leadership? To what extent did his church support missions? How the candidate's previous church approached evangelism is a crucial issue a conscientious search committee should explore.

IV. Examine the candidate's education

A pastor's education is important. If no one on the committee is familiar with theological degrees, then enlist an outside consultant who can evaluate the candidate's academic qualifications.

Take note of the degrees he earned. Some resumes state, "Studied at . . ." This phrasing usually indicates the applicant didn't finish the program. Perhaps he took one class or dropped out partway through his studies. Failure to complete a degree is a red flag. It could demonstrate a tendency not to persevere through challenges. Perhaps he struggled with the assignments or is a poor reader. Academic shortcomings bode poorly for someone who is expected to study and prepare solid sermons. There are numerous ways to earn degrees online or part time. Avoid hiring someone who doesn't finish what God leads him to start.

If the candidate completed his education, the type of degree he has is important. Churches might admire a pastor who earned a doctor's degree, but there are several types of doctorates. The two most common ones in ministry today are the Ph.D. (Doctor of Philosophy) and the D.Min. (Doctor of Ministry). The Ph.D. is the standard degree with the most rigorous academic requirements. Students typically study one or two foreign languages and write an extensive dissertation. A Ph.D. is not for the faint of heart and often requires full-time study to complete. If someone intends to find a job as a professor, he may seek a reputable Ph.D. program to make him an attractive candidate. Conversely, a D.Min. is designed to prepare ministers for practical work in the church and is less demanding academically. It can be a useful degree, but many schools have launched D.Min. programs to generate more revenue. The market has been saturated and standards have fallen. Certain schools are notorious for their low requirements and fees. They tend to attract students who don't want to invest heavily in the process. Determine why the candidate earned the degree. Some people seek the prestige of being a "doctor." Others pursue an education for far more noble reasons.

The same principle applies to master's programs. An M.Div. is considered the standard theological degree for church ministers. It usually requires a minimum of three years to complete. Other types of graduate programs typically involve fewer requirements. They have their place, but people often choose them because they are easier, cheaper, and quicker to attain. Strive to understand what type of degree a candidate holds and how difficult it was to earn.

Familiarity with the candidate's alma mater may also reveal something about his theological leaning or ministry style. Some institutions are more conservative whereas others have a more liberal bent. Some have reputations for developing solid, effective pastors, while others are known for producing ministers who are critical of others and uncooperative. Of course, there are many reasons to attend a particular school. Perhaps he merely chose the closest one to where he was already ministering. Nevertheless, it's wise to understand what type of training your potential minister received.

V. Look at outside interests

Well-rounded ministers have hobbies and interests outside ministry. If a pastor can enjoy his preferred recreational activities in your area, he will be more likely to settle into a long and fruitful ministry. Of course, it's prudent to consider whether he pursues these interests to excess! Some pastors devote more time and energy to their hobbies than to their church. They may be extremely difficult to reach during hunting or fishing season. While it's beneficial for your pastor to enjoy living in your community, ministering to his flock ought to be his priority.

Pastors may also serve on the boards of other ministries. Some ministers sit on several committees in their denomination. They may be involved in ministries outside their church, such as caring for orphans in Africa. Perhaps the candidate is passionate about mission work, preaching revivals, or writing books. These activities can all reflect a talented minister who is much in demand. But it may be prudent to set limits on the amount of time he should devote to outside ministry, especially if doing so takes him away from his church. Some pastors grow bored with their church and become consumed with outside interests. Avoid those pastors.

VI. Check references . . . then check them again!

One practice many search committees neglect is thoroughly investigating references. Many churches have been mortified to learn troubling information about their new minister after he arrived on the field. In some cases, people who knew the pastor later shared that they would have warned the church had someone asked them. Sadly, speaking to references is a necessary part of the hiring process. Ministers naturally present themselves in a positive light. Some people want a job so badly that they misrepresent themselves in hopes of obtaining the position. It behooves your committee to investigate every reference listed on a resume and then some.

A. References the candidate lists

Begin by speaking to each reference the candidate provides. For a church leadership position, it's wise to require at least six. Insist that several come from his last place of ministry and that at least one has direct knowledge of his family. Be sensitive to the quality and variety of his references. Failing to include anyone from his previous place of employment is a red flag, as is listing a peripheral person in his former church but no leaders or staff members. Most people can find at least one individual who appreciates their ministry. Hopefully, key church leaders are in that group.

B. Ask for additional references

The references a candidate provides will include his most enthusiastic supporters, so it's wise to delve deeper. When interviewing each reference, ask if there is someone else who might be worth contacting. If you obtain a set of 6-8 names that match those the candidate provided, then you can have greater confidence in those sources.

C. Be persistent

Getting in touch with references can be challenging. They may not answer their phone or emails promptly. Don't give up! Refuse to move forward until you've spoken with each person on the list. You may need to tell the candidate that some of his references are unavailable and ask him to prod them to return calls or provide new references.

D. Maintain confidentiality

Sometimes references have important concerns to share, but they worry the candidate might find out what they tell you. They may fear legal action if their information costs the candidate the job. For these reasons and others, references may be reluctant to share their concerns in writing. They might prefer to speak over the phone rather than filling out a document or sending an email the pastor may later see. Always allow references to speak with you in an unrecorded phone conversation. It's far more important to learn the truth than to have an official record of the exchange.

E. Check with leaders in the area

If a local associational missionary or denominational leader knows the pastor, ask for his opinion. Is the applicant supportive of other ministers and churches in the area? Is his church vibrant and growing? What is his reputation? Are there any other potential references the committee should contact?

VII. Check social media

Most people are active on social media. Investigating the candidate's posts and profiles is a simple and fruitful part of the vetting process. Does he take the high road on controversial issues? Does he encourage friends and church members? Does he rant about politics? Does he use off-color humor? Does he obsess over sports or bad calls by referees? Does he circulate dubious news stories? Are his posts respectful to his wife and children? Many people have had job applications scuttled by a careless social media presence.

VIII. Beware of extensive plans listed on a resume

Many candidates lay out their philosophy of ministry on their resume. This practice can be helpful. Some candidates go even further and list extensive plans for their next church. Perhaps they are enamored with a certain church-growth method, educational system, or approach to evangelism. Ironically, many of the candidates who list these ambitions have never previously served as a senior pastor. Nevertheless, they may have come to certain convictions about methodology while in seminary. Other candidates like to impose all the programming from their previous church on their new congregation.

My suggestion for such resumes is simple: throw them away! Don't call a pastor who has all the answers before he knows what the problems are. He will likely attempt to force his methodology on your church whether it's God's will or not. Effective ministers understand that evangelism, discipleship, and missions are key components of a healthy church, but they also recognize that there are numerous approaches to those ministries. Churches are unique. It's crucial for a pastor to get to know the church before committing to a method.

A good interview question may be, "If we call you as our pastor, what are the first things you will do?" If he lists the programs and approaches he will implement, be cautious. A much more encouraging response is, "I will spend time praying for the congregation, getting to know its members, and learning its history as I seek God's will for the church in the days ahead."

Your congregation needs a pastor who doesn't assume he has all the answers before he arrives. Programs serve the people; people don't serve a program!

IX. Determine whether any significant issues have been overlooked

Though a candidate may not want to lead with troubling past or current struggles on his resume, he ought to disclose them early in the process. These matters include divorce, adultery, bankruptcy, or being charged with criminal activity. For your congregation's safety, investigate any allegation to ascertain whether it's valid. Claims of sexual misconduct in particular must be taken seriously. Merely relying on the candidate's assertion that he doesn't have a problem anymore is far from satisfactory. As a general rule, a criminal history ought to terminate someone's candidacy. While Christians believe in grace, senior pastors should be held to exceedingly high standards.

Attempted suicide is another pertinent topic. Clinical depression and suicide occur far too often among ministers, and your committee must address these issues during the interview process. God can heal people, but these battles often require significant divine intervention to overcome. The committee should ensure a candidate has truly regained his health before asking him to enter a rigorous new ministry position.

A word of caution: Some churches are so anxious to obtain a pastor they overlook any failing if the person is willing to accept the position. Acting out of desperation is a recipe for disaster. Consider a candidate with major issues in his past only if there is clear evidence supported by multiple reliable references that he has significantly changed.

Conclusion

Resumes may be only a few pages long, but they contain a wealth of important information. Study them carefully. Diligently pursue any questions that arise. Your congregation is counting on you to find the person God has selected for your church.

CHAPTER 8

Narrowing the Field

We once heard a story of an engineer who felt he was too busy to sort through the resumes his office received for a job opening in the company. His associate grew exasperated as the pile continued to grow. Finally, the engineer grabbed the top half of the resumes from his desk and dropped them into the garbage can. As his associate's jaw dropped, the engineer declared, "Those people are unlucky. We don't need unlucky people working here."

While I don't endorse the engineer's method, reading through every resume and accompanying letter can quickly become tedious. Establishing some basic qualifications to narrow the scope of the search is appropriate and often necessary. The goal at this stage of the process is to determine which candidate to pursue further.

I. Watch out for these issues

Keep the following general guidelines in mind when determining who not to consider.

A. People who pressure the committee

Applicants may be anxious for updates on your progress. While curiosity is natural, some people may succumb to the temptation to contact you frequently for information. They might go so far as to pressure you to process their application. Anyone who pesters committee members should be taken out of consideration. Such behavior reflects a lack of trust in the Lord's leading and a deficiency of self-control. These candidates prove at the outset that they don't possess the character, walk with God, or people skills necessary for the job.

B. Candidates with questionable material on their resume

The first resumes to be culled ought to be those containing dubious material. Perhaps the candidate has struggled to hold down a ministry job or not completed his education. Perhaps he has a criminal record or is under investigation. Set a high standard for your next minister and sift out those who are unable to meet it.

C. Candidates who don't meet pre-specified qualifications

If your committee has deemed certain qualifications non-negotiables, be firm in rejecting candidates who don't possess them. For example, you might choose not to consider applicants who belong to a different denomination, don't list at least four years of related experience, are single, or don't have a master's degree.

II. Characteristics to note

After removing resumes that fail to meet the basic requirements, you must begin the harder work of considering stronger applicants. Look for these characteristics as you narrow your search.

A. Happy in his current position

One of the most important things to consider is the candidate's status at his present job. Is he content? Has he experienced success? Would people be sad if he left? Has he received any promotions? Look closely because you may be getting a glimpse into your future.

B. Reluctance to leave

A candidate may be hesitant to leave his present position. Don't be alarmed. Reluctance to change jobs is generally a positive sign. It indicates he is committed to the people he serves. Some pastors must be approached several times before they finally consider moving to a new church.

C. Restlessness or a sense his work is done

A pastor may feel as if his work is done. Perhaps he accomplished the major tasks God gave him and is ready for a new challenge. Some pastors are skilled at transitioning churches. Others are gifted at working with small congregations but struggle when their flock grows larger. Pastors may develop a strong, healthy church and feel ready for a new challenge. They may not recognize this restlessness themselves, but their wife, staff, or colleagues might. Search committees can often benefit from asking trusted ministers if they are aware of a skilled pastor who may be entering into a time of transition.

D. A background that matches your church's needs

When examining resumes, you will likely find many gifted leaders. But which person is ideally suited to meet your church's needs?

Perhaps your church senses it has outgrown its facility. Your previous pastor believed he was unqualified to spearhead a major building program, so he moved to a church that didn't require one. You might feel led to consider candidates with experience leading churches through building campaigns.

Maybe your previous pastor grew your church to the point that it required additional staff, but he was uncomfortable leading a multi-staff ministry and left for a smaller congregation. God might lead you to look for a candidate who has an aptitude for developing a church staff.

Your pastor might have left because he was unable to take the church any further. Rather than hiring a replacement who is just like him, choose someone who can address the issues your church will face in the future.

E. A clear sense of God's leading

You should seek someone who feels God unmistakably leading him to your church. As you investigate candidates, look for signs of God's activity in their life.

III. Practical guidelines to follow when identifying a leading candidate

Narrowing the field is one of the most difficult parts of the hiring process. Even after eliminating obviously unsuitable applicants, you may still have a dozen or more appealing candidates. Selecting the right person requires paying careful attention to God's leading.

A. Pray

Bathe everything you do in prayer. You may still have a significant number of viable candidates to investigate. Consider spending a week praying over the remaining resumes. Ask God to help you discern which qualifications are most important.

B. Narrow to three

Perhaps one person clearly stands out from the rest at this point, and you are ready to pursue him further. More often, several candidates look promising. In that case, narrow your search to the top three. Each one will have strong skills and many positive characteristics. Interview them or listen to them preach. The goal is to scrutinize each person until one emerges as the frontrunner.

Though you will be excited to reach this important milestone, maintaining confidentiality is prudent:

- Don't tell any applicant the names of the other candidates.
- Don't ask the candidates to preach at your church. The search process is not a preaching competition.
- Don't ask your church to choose between the three. It's better to set up private interviews with each one. If you bring the candidates into your city, meet them at a neutral site, such as a hotel. You may give them a tour of your facility during the week, but don't introduce them to the congregation yet.

C. Narrow to one

Some search committees mistakenly pit the three candidates against each other in an unofficial competition. Other committees are indecisive and keep three people in play for too long. At some point, you must identify a leading candidate. Narrowing to one person doesn't guarantee you have found your next pastor; it simply means you have determined which candidate the Lord is leading you to pursue first.

If you have not yet visited your leading candidate's church, do so now. Some committees tell the pastor when they are coming, but visiting anonymously may provide a more accurate picture of a typical service. If you choose to attend secretly, avoid wearing power suits and conspicuously sitting together in the auditorium. Doing so could create consternation among the congregation.

In addition to hearing the candidate preach, you should spend time with the pastor and his spouse in an informal setting. Some committees simply complete this step when the candidate visits in view of a call. The problem with this approach is that if the committee learns something troubling during their interactions with the candidate, walking back the process may be awkward. Do as much work as possible before introducing a candidate to the congregation.

D. Complete due diligence

Due diligence involves running a criminal background check and a credit check. Hopefully a candidate who has reached this stage of the search doesn't have any major skeletons in his closet. Unfortunately, some congregations have discovered that the pastor they just hired was under investigation for criminal activity or had experienced serious financial problems. Services are available to help you conduct these searches.

E. Decide whether to proceed

Once you have met with a candidate, listened to him, and prayed over him, it's time to decide whether to proceed further. Choosing not to pursue him is a legitimate decision. Heed any red flags that pop up, even at this late stage of the search. Perhaps the committee feels uneasy about the candidate. Maybe he checks all the boxes, but no one is excited about him. If you feel hesitant about moving forward, you owe it to the candidate to release him from your search.

After all the committee members have had ample time to vocalize their impressions and concerns, take a vote.

If it passes, then it's time to move on to the next step in the process.

Conclusion

These steps are similar to running a marathon. As the end of the race nears, you may feel weary and be anxious to finish. But this is not the time to grow careless or rush the process. There is still important work to do.

CHAPTER 9

Interviewing the Candidate

A resume may disclose a great deal about a candidate. Watching him preach can reveal even more. But at some point, a formal interview is in order. This chapter will outline ways to fully utilize that important tool.

I. Timing of the Interview

Some search committees schedule a stand-alone interview. Typically, the candidate and his wife meet with the committee privately in the city where the church is located. If the interview goes well, the committee schedules a time for the candidate to return to preach in a worship service.

A second option is to schedule the interview for the visit in which the candidate preaches at the church. Many committees choose this method to save money on travel expenses. For example, the candidate may be interviewed on Friday evening and then preach in a service later that weekend.

Although both approaches are common, the first is preferable. Once a candidate has preached before the church, some people will be eager to extend a job offer. It's wise to introduce the candidate to the church only after you have interviewed him and determined to proceed to the next step.

II. The Interview

Formal interviews provide a unique opportunity to learn about the candidate, his character, and his beliefs. For the interview to be effective, proper preparation is crucial.

A. Prepare the setting

The setting should be conducive to a successful meeting. A board table is often helpful so everyone can see the candidate and take notes easily. The room should be private and free from outside noises. Provide comfortable seating. Remove distracting signs or lists from whiteboards. Strive to make the room smell nice, perhaps with a diffuser or fresh flowers (but be sensitive to possible allergies).

B. Allow sufficient time

A thorough interview may take from one to three hours. It's best to allow for three hours and to cut the session short if appropriate. Don't feel compelled to fill the time after covering every pertinent topic. People are rarely disappointed when a meeting finishes early.

C. Prepare the agenda in advance

For optimal time management, put together a schedule for the meeting. Determine what topics you plan to address and allot sufficient time for each one. Sharing the agenda with the candidate in advance is not mandatory but often appreciated.

D. Ask effective questions

Though the interview can be one of the most useful steps in the search process, committees often ask surface-level queries that don't encourage thoughtful responses. Formulating deep, probing questions is the key to conducting a successful interview. Keep these guidelines in mind as you prepare:

1. *Don't ask questions that are too basic or broad.* Questions like, "Do you believe in prayer?" or "What do you think about evangelism and missions?" are largely useless. Of course he believes in prayer and missions! Believing in something and doing something are entirely different matters. How he addressed issues in the past is the best gauge of how he will handle them in the future. For example, rather than asking what he thinks about prayer in the church, ask about his experience with prayer: "Tell us about your personal prayer life. What answers to prayer have you recently

received? What did you do to promote prayer in your last church?" These questions may elicit a more enlightening response.

2. *Avoid hypothetical questions.* Again, determine what he has done about issues, not merely what he thinks about them. Don't ask, "How would you resolve conflict in the church?" A more effective line of questioning is, "Tell us about a time you experienced conflict in your church and how you resolved it." Everyone has ideas about what they would do, especially recent seminary graduates. But believing in conflict resolution isn't the same as having conflict-resolution skills.

3. *Ask about important issues his resume left out.* Perhaps his resume didn't mention mission trips or giving. A committee member might ask, "I didn't see anything about mission activities on your resume. Is missions a priority for you? If so, tell us about ways you led your church to be involved in missions." If he confesses that missions wasn't a priority in his last church, ask why. People typically devote time and resources to activities that are important to them.

4. *Ask open-ended questions.* If a question can be answered with a simple "yes" or "no," then there is probably a better way to phrase it. Ask open-ended questions that draw out deep, full responses.

5. *Ask his spouse questions.* Even though the candidate's wife is not being hired, her support is

vital to her husband's success. Speaking with his wife is also a good way to measure the health of a candidate's home life.

- *Discuss her participation in the church.* One way to estimate how involved she will be in your church's ministries is to ask, "In the past, what responsibilities has God led you to take on in your church as a pastor's wife?" While her participation may greatly bless your congregation, keep your expectations realistic.

- *Gauge her support for the potential move.* Although the candidate may be intrigued by serving in a new church, his wife might be upset at the thought of leaving her home and friends. She may live near her parents and be hesitant to move to a different state. Perhaps she has a successful career and feels conflicted about transferring to a new city. The move could result in a strained marriage if both parties aren't on the same page. It might be wise to ask, "What would be most difficult for you if you were to come to our church?"

- *Notice any tensions in the candidate's marriage.* A sensitive but revealing question to ask the couple is, "Have you ever sought marital counselling?" Ministry marriages often face enormous pressure. If there are fissures in their relationship, ministry demands can make them worse. Seeking counselling doesn't always indicate that a relationship is troubled. Perhaps they are proactive about addressing marital concerns. But if they have suffered from chronic problems throughout their marriage, take note. Moving to a new church and city can cause enormous pressure, and you should be aware if their relationship is vulnerable to it.

- *Discuss the children.* Moving to a new city will not only affect the couple but also their children. The candidate and his wife may have additional concerns if their child receives specialized care in school or through programs. The more you know about the minister's home life, the better you can care for his family.

- *Ask about her experience in her last church.* A general principle is that if the pastor's wife loved the people in her previous church, she'll grow to love the congregation at her next one. If she was never close to anyone in her last church, she probably won't develop strong ties to the people in your church either. An interesting question might be, "Tell us about some of your closest friends in your current church."

6. *Ask challenging questions.* Starting the interview with inquiries that are relatively easy to answer can break the ice and put the candidate at ease. But as the interview progresses, ask deeper questions that shed light on his character or walk with God. Consider the following examples.

- *Tell us of a mistake you made in ministry and how you would handle the situation differently next time.* Warning! If he can't recall anything he's done wrong, you've just uncovered a huge red flag! Every minister makes mistakes. The key is whether he admits to them, grows from them, and learns how to handle situations better in the future. Struggling to answer the question could signal insecurity or an inability to take responsibility for his shortcomings.

- *Where do you struggle in your Christian walk?* Watch how the candidate responds. Does he get defensive or is it clear that he regularly battles his shortcomings in an effort to become fully surrendered to Christ?

- *Why would you be willing to leave your present place of ministry?* If God called him to his current assignment, why is he considering leaving it? Has he finished everything God called him to do there?

- *How do you feel God has prepared you for service with us?* His answer may reveal how well he knows your church and whether his skill set is conducive to meeting its needs.

- *How would you respond if we don't feel led to proceed with you?* His response might indicate how strongly he feels led to your church. Is it just a job for him or does he clearly sense God drawing him to serve with you?

- *What concerns or questions do you have about our church?* The issues he raises could expose his priorities. For example, he may ask several questions related to a financial document you provided. He might be interested in the church's demographics or mission statement. If he has no questions or concerns, perhaps he hasn't done his homework or wants the job at any cost.

- *How might we make this transition easier for your family?* He may be apprehensive about the timing. Perhaps his wife will stay behind until their child graduates from high school the following spring. He might have made some commitments to his current church through the summer that he feels obligated to complete. Try to be flexible and make the transition as seamless as possible.

E. Investigate the tenure of his previous assignments

It's always wise to learn why a pastor left previous positions. Bouncing from church to church may reflect a character flaw. Perhaps he is unable to cooperate with others or is merely on the hunt for a better paying position. If a pastor has a history of short tenures, find out why:

- *Why did you leave your last two churches after only two years?*
- *Do you feel you accomplished all God intended when he called you there?*

- *How did your leaving affect the church?*
- *What confidence should we have that you would not leave us in two years?*

F. Read between the lines

Astute search committees pay attention to the candidate's body language, attitude, and behavior. Observing both verbal and nonverbal cues can provide a more robust picture of the candidate's character.

- *Does he talk too much?* How succinct and relevant are his answers? Does he chase rabbits? Does he listen carefully and answer questions directly?
- *Is he nervous?* An interview is an intimidating experience. Hopefully the candidate stands up well under pressure. Does he look people in the eyes when he talks with them? Does he get defensive? Does he appear confident and genuine?
- *How does he treat his spouse?* Does he pay attention to her? Does he ensure she has what she needs, such as something to drink? Do they ever appear to disagree on an answer? Does his wife talk too much? Is she engaged in the process?
- *Does he express interest in the committee?* Some candidates enjoy being the center of attention. Others naturally begin ministering to the committee even during the interview. Notice whether he remembers the committee members' names and asks about their lives and families. His

behavior during the interview may reveal a great deal about the kind of pastor he will be.

- *Does the candidate hold certain theological, social, or political beliefs that may divide your church?* Be sensitive to the positions the candidate takes on important or controversial issues. For example, he might have a certain strong theological position or a very conservative view of women's role in ministry. Perhaps his opinions on politics or social issues are divisive. While candidates are certainly free to have their own beliefs, beware of someone who holds or promotes divisive views that could detract from his ministry.

III. Debrief & Recommendation

As soon as possible after the interview, meet as a committee to debrief. Have everyone share their overall impressions of the candidate as well as any red flags they noticed. Afterward, vote on whether to introduce him to the congregation. If the vote passes, schedule a time for him to return to preach in view of a call.

Conclusion

You may choose to take a "dry run" of the interview. Determine which questions each committee member will ask. Consider the important issues. Be aware of the couple's needs. Prepare to be flexible if things become tense or emotional. Much rests on the outcome of the interview.

CHAPTER 10

Presenting the Candidate to the Church

After thoroughly vetting the candidate and conduct-ing a formal interview, it's finally time to introduce him to the church. Keep the following guidelines in mind as you prepare for this significant step in the pastor search process.

I. Treat the candidate with class and consideration

The way you treat your potential pastor will shape his opinion of your church. Attention to detail can ensure his visit is as pleasant as possible:

A. Encourage the candidate to bring his wife with him.

B. Provide all the information they need for their trip. Answer questions promptly and thoroughly.

C. Provide an expense form and reimburse any travel expenses he incurs.

D. If air travel is required, book a reasonable itinerary on a reputable airline so he arrives rested and prepared for the interview.

E. Put the candidate and his spouse up in a hotel room. The hotel should be quiet, comfortable, and offer onsite dining so they don't have to leave the building for meals. Do *not* house them in someone's home. If you do, they may feel obligated to visit with their host. They might worry about dirtying the bathroom, making too much noise, or leaving the bed sheets in disarray. A hotel room offers a private place to rest.

F. Leave a welcome basket in their room. Find out in advance what their favorite beverages and snacks are and be sure to include them. This small effort goes a long way toward expressing love and thoughtfulness.

G. Offer to provide the couple with a car to use while they are in the city. If they prefer not to drive, arrange transportation to and from the hotel.

H. Don't overlook the candidate's spouse. Perhaps some of the ladies on the committee can do something special with her, such as taking her to a nice place for lunch or showing her points of interest in the city. The key is to make her feel like she is an important part of the process. She might be concerned about local schools. Be prepared to help her find whatever information she needs as she considers moving her family to your location.

I. If the couple brings their children, strive to make the experience enjoyable for them. Include kid-friendly items in the gift basket. Arrange for the children to go on a fun excursion, perhaps with some of the search committee members' children. Choose a hotel with a swimming pool. Help the couple's children develop positive feelings toward your church and city.

J. Don't overload the schedule. Sometimes churches want to maximize every moment of the visit, and the couple becomes physically and emotionally overwhelmed. Be sure to include downtime, especially before a major event. For example, if the candidate is preaching in the morning service and then attending a major lunch outing afterward, leave adequate space in the afternoon for him to rest.

II. Meet formally and casually

Incorporate both formal and informal events into the schedule. In candid moments, such as over dinner at a restaurant, a candidate may express himself in ways he might not around a boardroom table.

III. Protect the candidate from outsiders

Many church members will be eager to meet the candidate. Some will want to share their opinions or concerns with him. While most people are respectful and gracious, some may be less thoughtful. Take the following steps to discourage unwanted encounters:

A. Prohibit the congregation from contacting him outside of public meetings.

B. Don't disclose his hotel information.

C. Be sure a committee member is always by his side when he is visiting with people.

D. Intervene quickly if someone takes too much of his time or speaks inappropriately to him.

IV. Prepare the church

Publicize the date and schedule for the candidate's visit in advance. Provide a handout that includes a picture of the candidate with his family and outlines pertinent information about his life and ministry. Church members ought to be encouraged to pray for discernment and clarity as they prepare for the upcoming vote. Some committees encourage the congregation to study *Experiencing God* as they seek God's will on the matter. People should be kept well informed of what is happening.

V. Allow adequate time for the candidate's sermon in the morning service

Churches often want to put their best foot forward on the day the candidate preaches, so they pack the service full of special music, announcements, and extra prayers. But it's better to keep the program simple and allow plenty of time for the candidate to share from his heart.

VI. Schedule a time to interview the candidate in front of the congregation

Many churches schedule a time for the prospective pastor to share his testimony and philosophy of ministry during an evening service. Allow the pastor's wife to share her testimony too if she is willing. Some churches designate additional time for a Q&A with the pastor. To make the process as smooth as possible, ask people to submit questions in advance. A moderator can then read them during the public meeting and allow the candidate to respond. While people are generally well-intentioned, it's best to avoid "open mics." A moderator should keep the questions pointed, appropriate, and concise. He can also re-word or omit inappropriate questions.

VII. Schedule time for the congregation to pray before voting

Some churches ask the candidate to wait in a room on campus and vote immediately after the worship service. Other churches require a week to pass before voting. While either method can be successful, waiting to vote is preferable. If the outcome is negative or divisive, the situation may be awkward if the candidate and his wife are still on the church campus. If the vote passes, the candidate may feel pressured to accept the call on the spot.

Choosing a pastor is a momentous job, and the decision should be based on more than whether people enjoyed the candidate's sermon. Taking a week to pray over the matter allows time for the congregation to seek God's will.

VIII. Voting on the Candidate

In congregational settings, the committee must address several important issues prior to holding a churchwide vote.

A. *Give proper advance notice*

Church constitutions often spell out how much notice is required before taking a vote of this magnitude. Use every medium available to announce the upcoming vote. The more people involved in the process the better.

B. *Pray before voting*

Ask God to guide your church. Be clear that you are seeking God's will. When taking the vote, don't ask who is for or against calling the candidate. Ask, "After praying and seeking God's will, do you sense that the Lord is leading this candidate to be our next pastor at this time?" What matters is not people's opinion but God's will.

C. Take the vote by secret ballot

Some churches call for a show of hands or a voice vote. If all are clearly in favor, these methods may be acceptable. But if there is any question about the vote being unanimous, then opt for a secret ballot. Voting anonymously frees people to be honest without fearing retaliation or criticism. Votes may be cast using a physical ballot or electronically.

D. Don't allow absentee votes

It is best to limit the vote to those in attendance. During contentious votes, disgruntled members may recruit people to vote who no longer attend the church. This practice lends itself to abuse and politicizing.

E. Count the vote and announce the decision

Once the vote has been taken, tabulate the results immediately and make them public. People will be anxious to know the outcome as soon as possible.

F. Have a plan in place for every possible outcome

Some church constitutions mandate that a pastor receive a certain percentage of the vote before he can be called. This bylaw is typically put in place to prevent a pastor from coming to a church where a sizable minority opposes him. While this rule is wise in some ways, it can also become a roadblock. In divided churches, seeking an 80% vote may be nearly impossible to achieve.

The vote may unfold in one of a few ways:

1.   Unanimous or near unanimous vote

The best-case scenario is that the vote is unanimous. Pastors who receive a unanimous affirmation begin their tenure in the best possible position.

More often, a handful of negative votes are cast. Sometimes church members are confused by the question and mistakenly vote no. Perhaps a few voters are contrarian and oppose the majority out of principle. Others, for whatever reason, may not feel that the candidate is the best person for their church. Receiving a small number of negative votes for any of these reasons is common and rarely a reason to reverse course.

2.   90% in favor

If the vote is 90% in favor, the pastor has a solid majority. But be sensitive to those who voted against calling him. Perhaps communication was poor. Some people may have strong opinions about what they want in a pastor and feel dissatisfied with the candidate. Maybe a group of people, possibly from the same Bible study class, voted *en bloc* against the motion.

The celebration might need to be somewhat muted. Perhaps a committee member can offer a plea for everyone to come together as a family to make the next pastor as successful as he can be. If the 10% was opposed for a certain reason, consider letting the candidate know what their concerns were so he can address them.

3.   80% or less in favor

With this outcome, churches ought to take a sober look at what God is revealing. Perhaps a vocal minority wants to prevent the candidate from becoming the next pastor. A minority of 20% shouldn't dictate what the 80% do, but the search committee must consider what this vote indicates.

Having 20% or more vote against a pastor doesn't necessarily mean he is the wrong person, but it could indicate that a significant minority has not yet sensed God's leading. The search committee may need to pause, listen to concerns, and answer questions. Moving forward with this percentage of people opposed is unwise. Perhaps a different candidate would face less opposition. After further discussion, the naysayers may feel satisfied and vote in the affirmative. The key is to help people recognize God's will. The church will likely need to take additional time before it is ready to move forward in unity.

4.   Declined

Sometimes the church extends a call and the candidate declines. Perhaps he decided not to accept the position unless the vote was 90% or higher. Maybe he senses that the church isn't a good fit for him. The thought of moving his family could simply be too daunting.

If a candidate declines the offer, the church should recognize that the situation is not a setback but an opportunity for further clarification of God's will. Immediately return to God in prayer.

If you started with a list of the top three candidates, you may then choose to turn to one of the remaining two. Don't be hasty to extend an invitation to the next person on the list. Trust the Lord in the process, and don't be disappointed if there are a few surprises along the way!

Conclusion

Your work is not complete until a pastor is comfortably installed in your church. Innumerable obstacles and setbacks may occur along the way. Remain undaunted and confident that as you follow God's leading, he will eventually guide you to the person he knows is best for your congregation.

CHAPTER 11

Follow up with the Candidate

After a candidate accepts the invitation, you have a few final tasks to do before your job is complete.

I. Make the move as easy as possible

Strive to make the transition a positive experience for everyone involved. Relocating and starting a new position is difficult and can elicit a wide variety of emotions. Your pastor and his family must say goodbye to friends and perhaps relatives. His wife might be leaving her job. The couple may need to sell their house and find a home in your community. Their children will likely be enrolling in new schools. At the same time, your pastor must write new sermons and get up to speed on church matters. The pressure can become overwhelming, especially if the congregation expects him to charge out of the gate fully prepared. Take the lead on lessening the burden on your pastor's family.

A.   Pay for your pastor and his wife to return to the church's city prior to their move so they can shop for a house and visit schools. Put them up in a hotel and provide a rental car if needed. The more tasks they can accomplish before arriving on the field, the sooner they will be ready to serve the congregation.

B.   Pay for a moving company to transport their belongings. Ask them to provide quotes from three businesses and then choose the one that appears to provide the best value.

C.   Gather names and phone numbers for doctors, dentists, and hairdressers church members use and recommend.

D.   Collect information on schools they might want to consider for their children.

E.   When the pastor arrives, offer him the first week and Sunday off so he can focus on moving into his office and home without worrying about preaching and dealing with church business.

F.   Provide a welcome basket that contains goodies and gift cards to area restaurants so the family can eat out while setting up their house.

G. "Pound" the pastor's new home or office with groceries and special items donated by the congregation so the family's pantry is full.

H. Ask a family with kids the same age as the pastor's children to take them on an enjoyable outing while their parents unpack the house. If the pastor has teenagers, perhaps some of the youth group can "kidnap" them and take them to do something fun.

There are countless ways to let your pastor and his family know their new church treasures them.

II. Seek to bless the entire family through the process

Many churches focus on the pastor but neglect his family. Strive to do all you can to minister to the pastor's whole family. If he has children, consider having kids of a similar age write them a note welcoming them to their new home. Send them gifts. Be aware that they may be going through a difficult time leaving their school and friends. Place each child on your prayer list and encourage church members to pray for them by name during the transition.

III. If there is a delay before the candidate can arrive on the field, find ways for him to begin bonding with the congregation

Sometimes the pastor can't commence his new position immediately. Find creative ways for him to start connecting with church members in the meantime. It may be beneficial for him to send an occasional video updating the congregation on how he is doing and offering prayers for the church. Doing so enables him to bond with his flock before he arrives on the field.

IV. Commit to being an ongoing support

Even after your search committee disbands, you can play an important role as advocates and prayer warriors for your pastor. Having been so intricately involved in the hiring process, you have a vested interest in helping him succeed. Pray for him regularly. Send him encouraging notes. It's important for members of the search committee to support the pastor even years into his tenure.

Conclusion

Churches are most likely to be healthy when they are led by godly, effective pastors. If your congregation is seeking a pastor, do all you can to find the person God has chosen to lead your church. Looking back on your life investments, serving on a pastor search committee may be one of the highlights.

Sample Prayer Guide for the Congregation During Search Process

As our church seeks God's heart and mind for the days ahead, we invite you to join the pastor search team in prayer. We encourage you to take time each day to focus on one of these specific prayers. We believe God will use this time of transition to unite our hearts and prepare the church for His next leader.

*Trust and patience in the midst of the transition...

> *"Trust in the Lord with all your heart, and lean not on your own understanding. In all your ways acknowledge Him and He will direct your paths (make your paths straight)."* Proverbs 3:5-6

*Acknowledge that only God can reveal what we need to know for today and the future...

> *"Call to me and I will answer you and show you great and mighty (unsearchable) things which you do not know."* Jeremiah 33:3

From that time many of His disciples went back and walked with Him no more. Then Jesus said to the twelve, "Do you also want to go away?" But Simon Peter answered Him, "Lord, to whom shall we go? You alone have the words of eternal life."

John 6:66-68

*For God to work in our hearts so we may know Him more fully, more deeply. . .

"...that you, being rooted and grounded in love, may be able to comprehend with all the saints what is the width and length and depth and height – to know the love of Christ which passes knowledge; that you may be filled with all the fullness of God."

Ephesians 3:17-19

"...that the God of our Lord Jesus Christ, the Father of glory, may give you the spirit of wisdom and revelation in the knowledge of Him, the eyes of your understanding being enlightened; that you may know what is the hope of His calling, what are the riches of the glory of His inheritance in the saints, and what is the exceeding greatness of His power toward us who believe..."

Ephesians 1:17-19

*That God is honored in and through our lives in all we say and do. . .

"Now thanks be to God who always leads us in triumph in Christ, and through us diffuses the knowledge of His fragrance in every place."
II Corinthians 2:14

"And whatever you do in word or deed, do all in the name of the Lord Jesus, giving thanks to God the Father through Him." Colossians 3:17

*For God to use this time to build a strong sense of unity throughout the congregation. . .

"Now therefore, you are no longer strangers and foreigners, but fellow citizens with the saints and members of the household of God, having been built on the foundation of the apostles and prophets, Jesus Christ Himself being the chief cornerstone, in whom the whole building, being fitted together, grows into a holy temple in the Lord, in whom you also are being built together for a dwelling place of God in the Spirit."
Ephesians 2:19-22

"I, therefore, the prisoner of the Lord, beseech you to walk worthy of the calling with which you were called, with all lowliness and gentleness, with longsuffering, bearing with one another in love, endeavoring to keep the unity of the Spirit in the bond of peace." Ephesians 4:1-3

*That God would reveal the leader He has in mind for our church in His timing. . .

"that the God of our Lord Jesus Christ, the Father of glory, may give to you the spirit of wisdom and revelation in the knowledge of Him"
Ephesians 1:17

"For I know the thoughts that I think toward you", says the Lord, "thoughts of peace and not of evil, to give you a future and a hope. Then you will call upon Me and go and pray to Me, and I will listen to you. And you will seek Me and find Me, when you search for Me with all your heart."
Jeremiah 29:11-13

"For My thoughts are not your thoughts, nor are your ways My ways," says the Lord. For as the heavens are higher than the earth, so are My ways higher than your ways, and My thoughts than your thoughts."
Isaiah 55:8-9

"In this manner, therefore, pray: Our Father in heaven, hallowed be Your name. Your kingdom come. Your will be done on earth as it is in heaven"
Matthew 6:9-10

*That God would give the new pastor and his family peace and confidence that this is God's purpose for their lives and that they can trust Him to work out all the details of the transition. . .

"Be anxious for nothing, but in everything by prayer and supplication, with thanksgiving, let your requests be made known to God; and the

peace of God, which surpasses all understanding, will guard your hearts and minds in Christ Jesus."
Philippians 4:6-7

"Trust in the Lord with all your heart, and lean not on your own understanding; in all your ways acknowledge Him, and He will direct your paths."
Proverbs 3:5-6

ABOUT THE AUTHORS

 **Dr. Richard Blackaby** has been a pastor, a seminary president, and is currently the president of Blackaby Ministries International. He has coauthored numerous books with his father, Henry, including: *Experiencing God: Revised Edition, Spiritual Leadership: Moving People on to God's Agenda, Fresh Encounter, Hearing God's Voice, Experiencing God: Day by Day, Called to Be God's Leader: Lessons from the Life of Joshua, Being Still With God, God in the Marketplace* and *Flickering Lamps: Christ and His Church.* He also authored: *Putting a Face on Grace: Living a Life Worth Passing On, Unlimiting God, The Seasons of God, Experiencing God at Home, The Inspired Leader,* and *Rebellious Parenting: Daring to Break the Rules So Your Child Can Thrive* and *Living Out of the Overflow: Serving Out of Your Intimacy with God.* Richard works with Christian CEOs of corporate America and speaks internationally on various topics including spiritual leadership in the church, the home, and the marketplace.

You can follow him at:

Twitter: @richardblackaby
Facebook: **Dr Richard Blackaby**

 **Rick Fisher** serves as Vice President for Blackaby Ministries International. He and his wife Debbie, live in Easley, South Carolina and have two daughters, Jamie and Betsy, sons-in-law Rob and Lucas, and five grandchildren – Thomas, Ashley, Jase, Leighton and Gray.

Rick earned a BA in Religion from Gardner-Webb University and a Master's degree from Southern Baptist Theological Seminary. He has served 30+ years of ministry in the local church (18 years of that as Senior Pastor) and has been part of the BMI team since 2008.

Rick ministers to churches, associations and businesses with focuses in the areas of spiritual leadership, leadership development, Experiencing God, revival/awakening and prayer/prayer ministry. He is the author of *"From Generation to Generation: Building a Godly Legacy"* and co-author of the book, *"Developing a Powerful Praying Church"*.

You can follow him at:

Twitter: @rickfisher54
Facebook: **Rick Fisher**

Blackaby Ministries International (www.blackaby.org) is dedicated to helping people experience God. It has books and resources to assist Christians in the areas of experiencing God, spiritual leadership, revival, the marketplace, and the family. There are also resources for young adults and children. Please contact them at:

Facebook: Blackaby Ministries International
Twitter: @ExperiencingGod
Mobile App: Blackaby ministries int
Website: www.blackaby.org

WWW.BLACKABY.ORG

BLACKABY RESOURCES
To discover all the resources BMI offers please see
www.blackabystore.org

BLACKABY LEADERSHIP COACHING
Blackaby Ministries provides coaching-based solutions to challenges
faced by ministry and marketplace leaders. To learn more, go to
www.blackabycoaching.org

BLACKABY REVITALIZATION/REVIVAL MINISTRY
If you sense God wants more for your church than what you are
currently experiencing, we want to help.
www.blackaby.org/revitalization-revival/

THE COLLISION
God is actively at work in the lives of the younger generation and
Blackaby Ministries is stepping out to join in this exciting activity.
www.thecollision.org

BLACKABY BIBLE INSTITUTE
Our onlince classes will guide you to a deeper level in your
relationship with God than you have ever experienced before.
www.blackabyinstitute.com